THIS WALKER BOOK BELONGS TO:

_____

_____

_____

For Walter

First published in Great Britain in 2004 by Walker Books Ltd
87 Vauxhall Walk, London SE11 5HJ

2 4 6 8 10 9 7 5 3 1

© 2004 Kathy Caple

The right of Kathy Caple to be identified as author/illustrator of this work has been asserted
by her in accordance with the Copyright, Designs and Patents Act 1988

This book has been typeset in Stone Sans

Printed in Singapore

British Library Cataloguing in Publication Data:
a catalogue record for this book
is available from the British Library

ISBN 1-84428-168-X

www.walkerbooks.co.uk

Worm Gets a Job

Kathy Caple

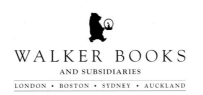

WALKER BOOKS
AND SUBSIDIARIES
LONDON • BOSTON • SYDNEY • AUCKLAND

Suddenly, it hit him.

Worm pushed the buggy towards the park.

When they reached the top, Worm stopped to rest.

Finally, Ronnie stopped crying.

But then, the buggy started to roll.

Worm caught the buggy and held on.

Worm headed straight over to Rat's house.

Worm knocked on Stinky's door.

Worm looked at Stinky's bedroom.

Next, Worm started on the living-room.

Worm vacuumed up a sock. He vacuumed up a banana skin.

He vacuumed up a handkerchief and an old sandwich.

Just then, Stinky walked in with Aunt Fussy.

Turtle scooted by on his newspaper round.

Worm stopped at the first house and threw the newspaper at the door.

He went to the second house and threw the newspaper.

He went to the third house and threw the newspaper.

He went to Turtle's house and threw the newspaper...

Worm's customers were ready to throw *him*.

Worm stopped at Frog's fruit stand.

Worm went to see Frog.

Frog showed Worm his work area.

**Worm went straight to work.
He painted the first sign.**

He painted the next sign.

Worm painted and painted. He threw himself into his work.

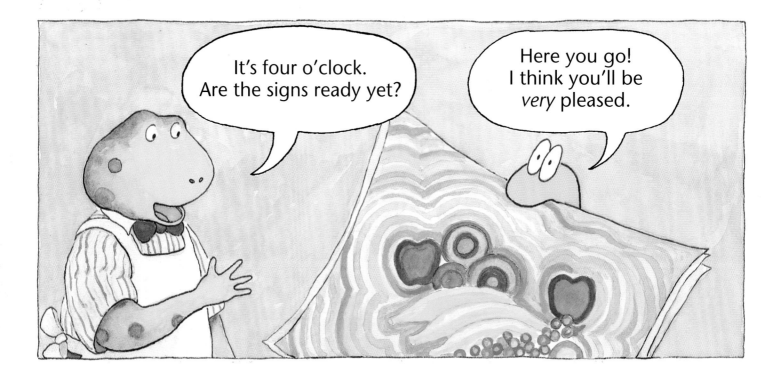

Next door, the judges from the art contest were standing outside.

Worm went up to accept his award.

When he got home, Worm painted and painted.

Then he had an idea.

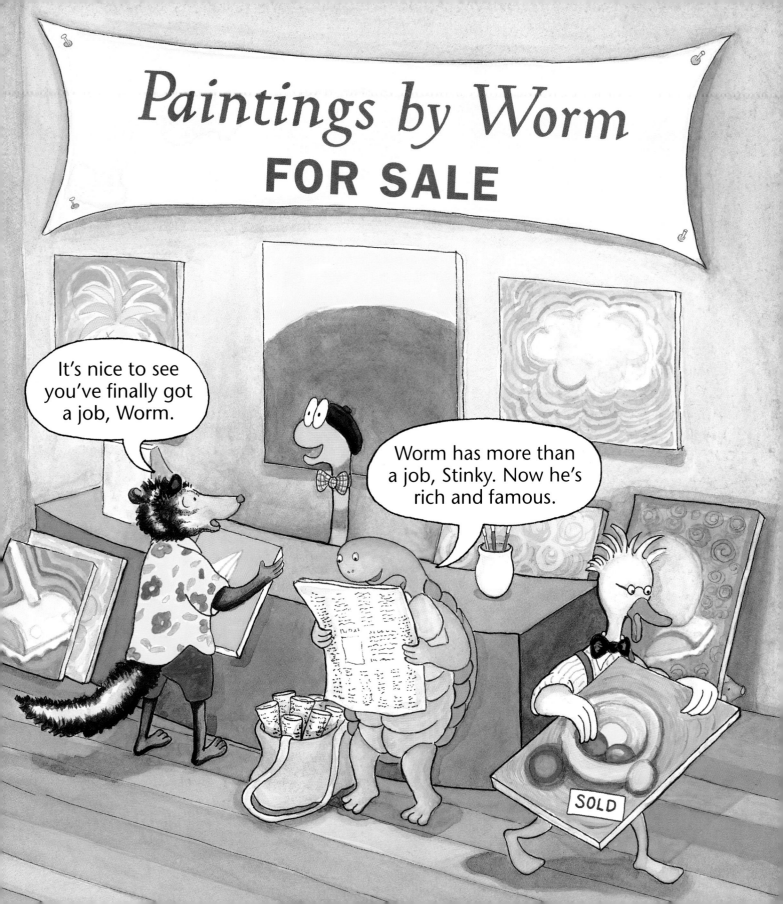

WALKER BOOKS is the world's leading
independent publisher of children's books.
Working with the best authors and illustrators
we create books for all ages, from babies
to teenagers – books your child will
grow up with and always remember. So…

FOR THE BEST CHILDREN'S BOOKS,
LOOK FOR THE BEAR